CONTENTS

Worship connects with the God who, through Jesus, transforms us and the world.

HEADLINES

Headlines make or break a newspaper. They catch the eye, draw the reader into the story, and engage the brain. The more a writer, journalist or publicist can make their work stand out, the more chance it will be picked up and read. How, for example, would the headline 'Bishop blasts shoddy services' grab a congregation? How would you react – denial or determination to do better?

Let's be honest. What headline is a journalist more likely to pick up from the conversation over coffee in church: one about the wonder of worship or one about house prices, the price of petrol or the weather? The trouble is that most Christians don't see worship as worthy of conversation, let alone headlines. They should.

Worship can be energizing, exciting, moving, mysterious and yes, even headline-grabbing: think back to the Archbishop of York at Easter in 2006, staging total immersion baptisms outdoors. But it can also be dull, pedestrian, lifeless. Why? In some churches, worship is brilliantly well planned and carried through, in others it is bland and boring: little thought is put into planning, even less into its effect on new worshippers. The emphasis is all on getting it done, not on how well it is done. Worship is vitally important. It should honour God and, like a newspaper headline, grab people, engage them and change their lives. It should inspire and excite. It is the heart of a church. Worship is the Church's 'headline business'.

This booklet isn't just for clergy or academics or people with a special interest in liturgy and ceremonial. It is for everyone who worships, to help each one look again at what we are doing when we worship God. Worship lies at the heart of what and who we are as Christians: it shows God to us and us to God.

Worship transforms us as individuals and as a community:

- We **belong** to God and to each other in the worship we share.

- We **become** the people God wants us to be through worship.

- We **believe** in God and that belief is shaped by our worship.

What about your place of worship? What headline would you write that compels the reader to read on? Could your worship – informal, solemn, traditional or contemporary – be better? For God's people, a dull headline will not do.

HARD-WIRED FOR WORSHIP?

Babies as young as six weeks often take to water as the most natural thing in the world, without the fears of older children and adults. Learning to swim when we are older is a different matter. We're afraid of the water, we daren't take our feet off the bottom. We need to overcome our fears and rediscover that water keeps our bodies afloat – whatever our shape or size.

Worship – when humans meet the divine – is natural, yet entirely new, even strange, to those who discover it for the first time. The core of our being is drawn towards God. Such encounters aren't confined to organized worship – in church services, at prayer retreats or at large Christian conferences. They can and do happen anywhere. We instinctively respond to signs that God is present and at work in the world around us, even when we don't fully recognize that it is God. We may not literally fall down on our knees but we do respond naturally to beauty, love and compassion. When we experience these, we experience something of God.

But worship is also an art and sometimes the canvas is blank and needs work. You rarely find someone who always feels like worshipping God. The fact is that most of us have to give time to it, if we are to learn to do it well.

Anyone in a loving relationship knows there are ups and downs, times when you don't feel as strongly attracted. Willpower and determination keep the spark alive. Relationships take time, space and energy to flourish. It's no different with worship – we need to learn how to worship, to grow in our relationship with God, and not just go with the flow, because the flow can ebb away.

Almighty God, you have made us for yourself,
and our hearts are restless till they find their rest in you:
pour your love into our hearts and draw us to yourself,
and so bring us at last to your heavenly city
where we shall see you face to face;
through Jesus Christ our Lord.

Common Worship,
Collect for the Seventeenth Sunday after Trinity

God is love and those who live in love live in God.

1 John 4.16b

GOD MEETS US

An encounter with God is not as unusual as you might think. The BBC's *Soul of Britain* survey (2000) found an astonishing 50 per cent increase in people's overall spiritual awareness over the past twenty years.

There are plenty of people in the Bible at a loss for words, too. Take Moses, not the most confident speaker. When he meets God in the burning bush there are no long speeches. Instead, Moses takes off his sandals: he knows he is on holy ground.

What is clear is that not everything depends on our ability to put things into words. God isn't waiting for

Why is good worship important?

us to make all the moves. Again and again he takes the initiative. Let's look again at Moses. It was God who came to him in the burning bush, not the other way round. And it was God who reached out to everyone through Jesus. To our surprise perhaps, God continues to invite each of us into a close relationship, a partnership. And when we don't know what to say or do in response, the Holy Spirit helps us. We may not always speak God's language but he speaks ours.

So what's going on when we gather for worship? As we hear the Bible read and we think together about what it means for us, God speaks to us. As we join with others to sing God's praise, as we kneel in silence to confess our failures, or clasp someone's hand to share God's peace, God reaches out to us. And we are changed.

WORDS

'You are what you tell yourself', if you believe the popular psychology in books and on the Internet. Repeating positive words in a certain way, the claim goes, affects our subconscious and makes those words come true: tell yourself you are healthy and happy – you become healthy and happy. It's a powerful claim and one that raises many questions. Whether it's true or not, words certainly have great power, for good or for ill. They can build us up or destroy us.

The Church has always recognized the power of words. Our faith grows out of the words of Scripture, and down the centuries we have struggled to find the right words to talk about God. Above all, words have a vital part to play in worship – to praise, to pray and to say what we believe. The words we use in worship matter.

But are there simply too many words, and do we repeat them too much? After all, didn't Jesus warn: 'In your prayers, do not go babbling on' (Matthew 6.7, REB)? In other words – be real with God and say what you mean. There's all the difference in the world, though, between meaningless repetition and a godly repetition that enables words to sink into us, and helps form us as Christians.

The apostle Paul wrote 'let the word of Christ dwell in you richly' (Colossians 3.16). One way is by becoming familiar with the words we use in worship; the words that come to have a deep and lasting effect on us. Repetition helps us take in and digest life-giving truths.

That might not sound very different from popular psychology. But it is. Words in worship point to something real beyond themselves – to God himself. And it's there that Christian faith and popular psychology part company. The words of worship are not merely our words – positive phrases we hope will make us feel better – but words forming part of an age-long and continuing conversation with the living God. When we regularly speak and sing certain words, they take root in us, but the power to change us comes from God alone.

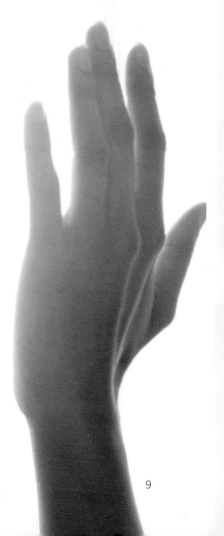

Faithful one, whose word is life:
come with saving power
to free our praise,
inspire our prayer
and shape our lives
for the kingdom of your Son,
Jesus Christ our Lord.

New Patterns for Worship

ACTIONS SPEAK LOUDER

Many of us are a bit floored when asked to do things in church. It doesn't matter whether it's shaking hands with the stranger next to us, joining in the actions for a children's worship song, walking in procession out of the building, having our feet washed or just putting our hands in the air – we feel awkward and reluctant.

Maybe it just doesn't feel 'British'. Or perhaps we think worship is a private matter. We may even think that public worship is actually a distraction from the real thing. Shouldn't it be what's inside us that matters rather than the actions we do?

But in the rest of life, don't actions speak louder than words? A friend who tells you they thought of getting a card for your birthday but didn't get round to it won't impress you when they add 'but it's the thought that counts'! Genuine faith involves responding with our mind, spirit and body. It's the whole of us that belongs to God and we need to respond to him with our whole being.

Regular actions can have a powerful impact on hearts and minds. Soldiers are drilled repeatedly on the parade ground so they will respond instinctively in the heat of battle. It's crucial for their survival. Regular involvement in worship is also crucial for Christians – it shapes us deep down. How many of us have gone to church not in the mood for worship, only to experience a U-turn simply by taking part? We felt we were just going through the motions, but there was more going on than we realized.

It matters whether we do things like standing, sitting, kneeling, or shaking hands with those around us in worship. These actions have a profound effect. Sometimes they challenge us to move out of comfort zones into new experiences and new attitudes. Sometimes we find them distracting. But don't be fooled: actions are never neutral.

What would Jesus think of your local church or place of worship?

REMEMBRANCE

Mel Gibson's controversial film *The Passion of the Christ* was a box-office triumph. Millions, of all faiths and none, queued to see it. Something about the life and death of Jesus drew them in. A story re-told over the centuries came powerfully alive and people were affected by it.

'Lord, remember me when you come into your kingdom,' said the thief hanging beside Jesus on the cross. It's one of those moments that strike a chord with so many of us. Presumably, he didn't mean: 'when you are in heaven enjoying yourself, stop for a moment, think about me, and then carry on happily with the party.' No: he hoped that, when Jesus thought of him, he would do something to change his situation, to save him. In the Bible, 'remembering' is a word that normally leads to action. In prayer and worship it usually does too.

When we stop and think of what happened to Jesus on the cross, we can feel great sorrow – human cruelty causing such suffering; Jesus dying a brutal death for the evil in men and women; because of us. But remembrance can also release something very powerful into our lives – the power of the victory of the cross. It comes home to us that Jesus has overcome the forces of evil. Jesus who suffered is also Jesus who conquered death, and through his Spirit he is present and able to save us now.

This happens when we listen to Scripture, when we sing hymns and songs, when we pray for those in need. Above all, it happens in Holy Communion when we obey Jesus' command to 'do this in *remembrance* of me'. His death long ago and far away becomes a present and powerful reality. His once-for-all sacrifice transforms us, and our lives, here and now. Remembrance has led to action.

Filled with the power of his Holy Spirit, we are sent out to live and work in his name, to continue his mission to save the world. Remembering is a word that leads to action. Death leads to resurrection.

What single thing would most revolutionise worship in your church?

CHURCH AND WORSHIP

'Live Earth', 'Make Poverty History', 'Live 8' – we are in the era of the big global event – nothing less will do than these vast concerts with their celebrities. However famous they are, those who perform know they are part of something much bigger – a movement, a huge and complex team – directors, producers, assistants, technicians, sound engineers, graphic designers . . . And in the end the success of the event is down to ordinary fans, the support they give and the attitudes and lives changed beyond the day itself.

Describing the Church as 'Team Jesus' might well make people bristle. But we are a team, a movement, a pilgrim people following Jesus Christ. And, when we worship together, each of us has a vital and unique role. Even if we think we are mere spectators or simply supporters, we are actively engaged in what is going on. Together, whatever our lives or backgrounds, we form a community when we worship together.

Whenever we meet around the font, we form a community with everyone baptized throughout the world, and throughout history. We belong to a very big team.

Whenever we gather around the Bible, we join with all those who read the Scriptures. We are with everyone discovering more about God and we learn from one another. We belong to a team of learners, of disciples, and those becoming disciples.

Whenever we get together for Holy Communion around the Lord's Table, we form a community with all who are fed with Christ's body and blood and we are sent out to make Christ known in our words and in our actions.

Whenever and wherever we meet, we are always worshipping with the church throughout the world and the whole company of heaven. Even if we are praying alone, we are never really on our own. We are always part of a team.

HOLY PLACES?

Are some places really more spiritual than others? Does where you pray or worship really matter?

The village of Walsingham in north Norfolk was recently voted the nation's most spiritual place in a BBC poll. A place of pilgrimage in medieval times, it continues to be valued as what some people call a 'thin place' – somewhere God's presence seems to 'leak' through more easily.

Places in the natural world can come to be seen in this way, too. And the Bible describes people having earth-shattering experiences of God on certain mountain-tops and other holy places. We don't always need a purpose-built church or grand cathedral to get in touch with God. Christians can worship almost anywhere – and do.

Many places built specially for worship provide the same feeling of peace and oneness with God. The skill of the architect puts across something of God's nature in the beauty or the splendour of the building. More often we sense the love that worshippers have lavished on the place and the prayer that has been offered there – sometimes for hundreds of years. That makes it feel holy and encourages us to join that worship.

Sadly, the opposite applies if a church seems neglected, suggesting that God, worship and love of neighbour do not matter there. An unloved church implies an unloved God.

An ordinary room, even a little corner, can become a sacred space and speak of the greatness of God's care for all if it is made holy by signs of loving worship.

Be still, for the presence of the Lord, the Holy One is here;
Come bow before him now with reverence and fear.
In him no sin is found, we stand on holy ground;
Be still, for the presence of the Lord, the Holy One is here.

SCRIPTURE

'The least read best-seller'? Many people own a Bible but never read it, and few would claim to really understand it.

For Christians, taking the Bible and its message seriously is bread and butter. All Christians need their own ways to read the Bible and absorb its message, such as a regular routine of prayer and study. But it is also vital to read the Bible during worship.

Reading the Scriptures is a reminder of the simple but profound truth that Jesus is with us. We hear the story of God with his people – a story that builds up to the climax of God breaking into history in an unexpected way by sending his Son as a human being.

This build-up is reflected in the order in which the Bible is often read in worship: Old Testament, New Testament, Gospel. The readings move with gathering momentum towards a 'head-on' encounter with Jesus in the words of the Gospel. In some churches, the Gospel is read from among the worshippers as a reminder that Jesus meets us face to face in worship.

The Bible in worship places God's story alongside our own and reveals Jesus as the one in whom those stories come together. We find a new place of belonging for our own lives, what we've experienced and where we're going. The written words of Scripture lead us beyond the page to 'the Word' who 'became flesh and dwelt among us'.

PUTTING ON CHRIST

Newsagents are full of magazines offering a variety of desirable lifestyles to which readers can aspire. Select the identity which most appeals and join a sort of consumer community. 'Who we are' today is largely a question of lifestyle choices – where we live, our job, what we wear, the food we eat, where we shop.

Lifestyle questions are significant. But Christians discover their truest identity not in these choices, but by 'putting on Christ' (Galatians 3.27), as Paul says. This means far more than adopting a particular lifestyle. It's about beginning a journey towards becoming the unique person God intends each of us to be. It's a journey we share with others in the family of the Church.

As many of you as were baptized into Christ have clothed yourselves with Christ.

Galatians 3.27

We 'put on Christ' when we are baptized. Baptism marks our identity as Christians. It is the way a person 'signs on the dotted line', declaring that they will follow Christ and take their place as a member of his Church. Hence, the actions and words of a baptism service:

- We are signed with the cross, the sign of Christ – an invisible 'badge' to show that we belong to Christ before anyone else.

- We – or our godparents on our behalf – make a public 'decision' to reject evil and to follow Christ.

- As we are dipped in water, or water is poured over us, it is as though we are passing through the waters of birth to begin a new life in Christ.

- At the end of the service, we are sent out with a lighted candle to show that we continue our journey in the company of Christ, the Light of the World.

Baptism happens to us only once. But we go on attending other people's baptisms throughout our life. Each time, we are reminded 'who we are' and where we belong within God's family.

Let us build a house where love is found
in water, wine and wheat:
A banquet hall on holy ground
where peace and justice meet.
Here the love of God through Jesus
is revealed in time and space;
As we share in Christ the feast that frees us:
All are welcome, all are welcome,
All are welcome in this place.

Marty Haugen copyright © 1994 GIA Publications Inc

FEEDING ON CHRIST

Only a third of British families eat together more than once a week, according to a recent survey. Some would call this a sign that society is breaking up and people are increasingly living their lives as individuals. Sharing food and drink lies at the heart of what it means to belong to a family or group of friends. Eating with people who matter to us is important. A meal together makes every person round the table feel included and valued.

The Church is Christ's family and sharing hospitality is one of the signs of a living congregation – a place where strangers are accepted and everyone is made truly welcome. At the heart of the gathering is a meal – the meal that Jesus himself gave us: the Holy Communion, the Eucharist, or The Lord's Supper.

Jesus is the host. He gathers us around his table. We remember all that Jesus did, his death and resurrection. But not only that, Jesus is present with us at the meal. He gives himself to us as food for our journey.

When the service is over and we go our separate ways, we still remain united to Jesus and to one another. We discover for ourselves the truth of his words:

Those who eat my flesh and drink my blood abide in me, and I in them.

John 6.56

Almighty God,
in Christ you make all things new:
transform the poverty of our nature
by the riches of your grace,
and in the renewal of our lives
make known your heavenly glory;
through Jesus Christ our Lord.

Common Worship, Collect for the Second Sunday of Epiphany

TRANSFORMING WEDDINGS

Some say marriage is only a piece of paper, so why bother? But anyone who makes such momentous promises in front of their family and friends knows that, from that moment, their relationship is changed.

Paul and Susan knew that marriage was a huge step to take. That's why they had been delaying. As the wedding drew near, the meaning began to dawn. They had read and re-read the words while organizing the service but now the time was upon them. This was their occasion. The Bridal March was over. They were in the spotlight, holding hands, with smiling rows of friends and family waiting expectantly for the couple to exchange promises in front of them and in the eyes of God. The words were much bigger than 'I love you' and those words were not normally exchanged in others' hearing.

Just a memorable and moving public ceremony? No. Relationships are cemented, two become one and the shape of two families is changed; and talk about God has a new dimension to it. Something more than simply signing the register happens at a wedding. It is a multi-layered event – with spiritual, emotional, relational, financial and domestic implications. Change takes place on many different levels.

And it's not just weddings that are transforming experiences. They are just one example of the many ways in which all kinds of worship can, and should, change people.

The God of heaven transforms our world when we gather and call upon him.

FROM DEATH TO LIFE

Peter Pan declared: 'To die will be an awfully big adventure.' For most people, death doesn't sound much like an adventure – more like a tragedy, a time of distress and loss.

Those left behind experience death as the departure of the deceased into the unknown, while they are left to forge a new path alone. People come to a funeral service with a whole mix of powerful emotions – pain, fear, regrets, guilt, anger. The service gives them space and time to acknowledge such feelings in words both spoken and heard. They get an opportunity to express their thanks for a life and a relationship shared. Finally, and most importantly, they say farewell to the person who has died.

Although it is the end of one journey, death is also the beginning of another – both for the person who has died and for those left behind. The funeral service helps bring about this transition for the bereaved.

Being able to acknowledge their sadness and loss openly is a first step forward. Admitting their hurts and asking for forgiveness begins a process of healing. Letting go of the physical remains and commending the person they have loved to God's mercy is starting a new journey.

This is a slow process. It will be accompanied by doubt and uncertainty. But the actions and words of the service should begin to provide mourners with some stirrings of comfort, assurance, even hope. A funeral brings about a significant change in their life's journey.

This is one of the most important things that any act of worship can – and should – do: to enable us to move from the old to the new. When we come out of a service, we should never be the same as when we went in; but ready to begin again what might after all turn out to be 'an awfully big adventure'.

WASH ME AND I SHALL BE CLEAN

The aftermath of a major oil spill creates some of the most dramatic pictures on our television screens. Beaches once covered only with golden sand are overlaid with thick black crude oil. Seabirds, caked with the toxic stuff, struggle to free themselves from its lethal grip, while others lie dead on the shore. Volunteers try to save those they can; others work to clean the sands and help the wildlife recover its habitat.

Life can do the same to people. Selfishness, greed, anger, hostility and other poisonous things are generated in our society and they stick to us. No special shower gel can wash it all away.

Adults who come new to faith are often aware of the contrast between who they have been and who God is calling them to be. They look forward to 'laying aside every weight and the sin that clings so closely' (Hebrews 12.1). The images used in the baptism service illustrate what happens to those who turn to Christ.

The service pictures the clinging grime of evil being washed away from the human heart to reveal once more the person created in the image of God.

We hear the story of God's people escaping from slavery in Egypt through the waters of the Red Sea to freedom in the Promised Land. It reminds us of our journey from being coated with sin, through the water of baptism, to a new life.

When those being baptized are submerged in the water before rising out of it, it is a dramatic expression of what the apostle Paul says about sharing spiritually in Christ's death and resurrection. The font is both a tomb in which we bury the old self and a womb out of which we are born anew.

Lotions and creams used after bathing protect and nourish the skin and smell good to others. When those being baptized are anointed with oil, we are reminded of the Bible's message about Christians being anointed with the Holy Spirit, as Jesus was at his own baptism, so that we may offer ourselves as a sweet-smelling sacrifice to God.

We have been buried with him by baptism into death,
so that, just as Christ was raised from the dead . . .
so we too might walk in newness of life.

Romans 6.4

YOU ARE WHAT YOU EAT

That's what diet gurus tell us. It makes you stop and think. Are we healthy, vibrant, happy people, filled with the latest so-called superfoods? Or does our food really depict us as convenient, pre-packed, fatty and sugary, or even just a little addicted to 'fast food'?

'You are what you eat' makes the point that our food has a powerful effect on our appearance, health and well-being. It also has a spiritual meaning for Christians, for whom eating and drinking have a profound importance.

In the celebration of the Holy Communion, we are fed by word and sacrament.

As we reflect together on the Scriptures, God's word feeds us and we are changed. We become more like Christ in our daily living. As we receive Holy Communion, we are spiritually nourished by Christ's body and blood. And we become what we eat. We are transformed into the body of Christ and sent out to do his work in the world.

Diet gurus, by the way, didn't invent the concept that we are what we eat. The great fifth-century theologian, Augustine of Hippo, said:

Through that bread and wine the Lord Christ willed to commend his Body and Blood, which he poured out for us unto the forgiveness of sins . . . you are what you have received.

Augustine of Hippo, *Sermon 227*

FORGIVEN AND FORGIVING

Do you know the famous sculpture called 'The Thinker?' But what is he thinking about? Maybe it's life's journey. Whenever we do that, looking back over many years or just the last week, there are always things we're not proud of. Changing that is a life-long challenge.

Paul knew that. He writes, 'I do not do the good I want, but the evil I do not want is what I do' (Romans 7.19). However hard we struggle to become more Christ-like, we cannot make ourselves perfect. Complete freedom from the burden of wrongdoing and wrong thinking can only be found in the forgiveness of God.

Admitting fault never comes easily, but this is the doorway to forgiveness. When we worship in church, we meet with others who know they are not perfect in God's eyes. So most services include a prayer of confession – a way of asking for God's forgiveness.

In the Confession we remember what is wrong in our own lives and what is wrong in our society, too: we don't only bear the scars of our own mistakes but we are damaged by those of others as well. Jesus teaches us:

Whenever you stand praying, forgive, if you have anything against anyone; so that your Father in heaven may also forgive you your trespasses.

Mark 11.25

The words of absolution that normally follow prayers of confession give God's assurance and forgiveness.

Our own wrong attitudes and actions, the evils of our society and the scars we bear from others can crush us. Every time we worship we can lay before God what weighs us down. Forgiven and forgiving, we can hold our heads high, renewed with those who worship alongside us to live like Christ. As we recognize this, our wounds are healed.

Christ crucified draw you to himself,
to find in him a sure ground for faith,
a firm support for hope,
and the assurance of sins forgiven . . .

Common Worship, Passiontide Blessing

PRAYING FOR OTHERS

Unlimited joy, health, money, relationships, love, youth: everything we have ever wanted – all these can be ours, according to a best-selling self-help book. Think positively about acquiring something, it claims, and you shall have it. Is that what prayer and intercession is about, like a divine shopping list? 'Dear God, we pray for this for him, and that for her, this for me and that for the other.'

True intercession is about solidarity, not wish lists. It grows out of our relationship with our heavenly Father and our love for one another. We pray because we love, not merely to acquire things.

In intercession, we admit our needs, name the needs of those we care for, and even of our enemies. Most importantly, we bring these needs to the one who wants to listen to our voice as much as we want to listen to him.

Intercession can be more than words alone. Paul describes how God's Spirit intercedes for us 'with sighs too deep for words' (Romans 8.26). An action, a gesture or a movement can sometimes express prayer far better than our words ever could.

Beside the candle-stands in many churches today we see a sign that says 'To light a candle is to pray.' To light a candle, to place a stone or to lay a flower within an act of worship provides an expression for prayer which does not need words.

So, while self-help literature offers a self-centred approach to life, based around what one critic has summarized as 'me' and 'stuff', to intercede is centred on God; 'bearing one another's burdens, and so fulfilling the law of Christ' (Galatians 6.2). When this happens, our dreams and desires are brought into harmony with God's objectives. We are transformed. We are changed from human beings who focus chiefly on ourselves, into those who share Christ's love for all creation.

Almighty God, who hast given us grace at this time with one accord to make our common supplications unto thee; and dost promise that when two or three are gathered together in thy Name thou wilt grant their requests: Fulfill now, O Lord, the desires and petitions of thy servants, as may be most expedient for them; granting us in this world knowledge of thy truth, and in the world to come life everlasting. Amen.

The Book of Common Prayer,
Prayer of St John Chrysostom

God of glory,
around whose eternal throne all the heavenly powers offer you
ceaseless songs of praise:
grant that we may overhear these songs,
and with our own lips and lives interpret them
to all in whose presence we play or sing;
that your Church may behold the beauty of its King,
and see with mortal eyes the land that is afar off,
where all your promises are celebrated,
and where all your love in every sight and sound
is the theme of eternal rejoicing:
through Jesus Christ our Lord.

Erik Routley

THE SOUND OF MUSIC

'Trendy priest sacks "out-of-date" choir' isn't such an uncommon headline; people hold strong opinions about music. Most discussion of music in worship tends to be about conflict over personal taste, or about styles and traditions: hymns *versus* worship songs, guitars *versus* organs, choirs *versus* praise bands, and so on. But this totally misses the point – music (whatever it is) plays a profound part in worship and is really about transformation.

Music helps build community. Whether we sing or play in a group or choir, or take part in congregational singing, we do so as the *whole* people of God giving voice in worship. When we share in music, we are changed from worshipping individuals into a worshipping people.

Music can lift our worship on to another plane. St Augustine wrote: 'the one who sings prays twice.' When we sing something, the words are transformed and their meaning is enhanced. What we sing, we tend to remember far more easily than words alone. Rhythm, melody, harmony and texture help us absorb words which lodge deep within us and shape us as Christians. How many times do we find ourselves humming or singing part of a hymn or song that we sang in worship last week? Music helps words that express the truth about God become part of us and feed us from within.

But music also has the power to help us 'draw near to God', to come into his presence, to 'log on to the worship of heaven'. It's not for nothing that many of the pictures of heaven in the Bible are of people singing, together, around God's throne. Music – of whatever tradition – can help do this, and in bringing us closer to God, can give us a glimpse of his glory and open us to being transformed by his love.

CREED

Most of us have a favourite song, and couples often have one they call 'our song'. So do other groups of people – think of school songs, for instance, or the chants of football or rugby team supporters. Even if you're not a football fan, you've only got to hear 'You'll never walk alone' and a particular team probably comes to mind. Songs can identify us, say who we are, and their words say something about the sort of person or people we believe ourselves to be. In other words, they are part of our personal creed, for that is what a creed does – says who we are and what we believe.

A creed is a standard ingredient in Anglican worship. But we also express our faith in other ways. We do so by the hymns and songs we sing, and the prayers we say. But above all we reveal our faith by just being there. We express to others our continuing faithfulness to the Christian gospel by persevering in prayer and worship week after week, day after day. In fact, the whole of our worship reveals our Christian identity.

Our worship not only reveals our identity but turns us into the people God wants us to be. The words we hear and speak gradually shape who we are.

That's why getting our worship right is important.

Bad worship will not identify us as good disciples of our Lord: bad worship distorts our identity as God's people.

he only Son of God,
ternally begotten of the Father,
od from God, light from light,
rue God from true Go
egotten, not made,
f one Being with the
hrough him all things
or us and for our salv
e came down from h
as incarnate of the H
nd became truly hum
or our sake he was cr
e suffered death and
n the third day he ros
n accordance with the
e ascended into heave
nd is seated at the righ
e will come again in
nd his kingdom will ha

e believe in the Holy Spirit, the Lord,
ho proceeds from the Father [and the S
ho with the Father and the Son is worsh
ho has spoken through the prophets.

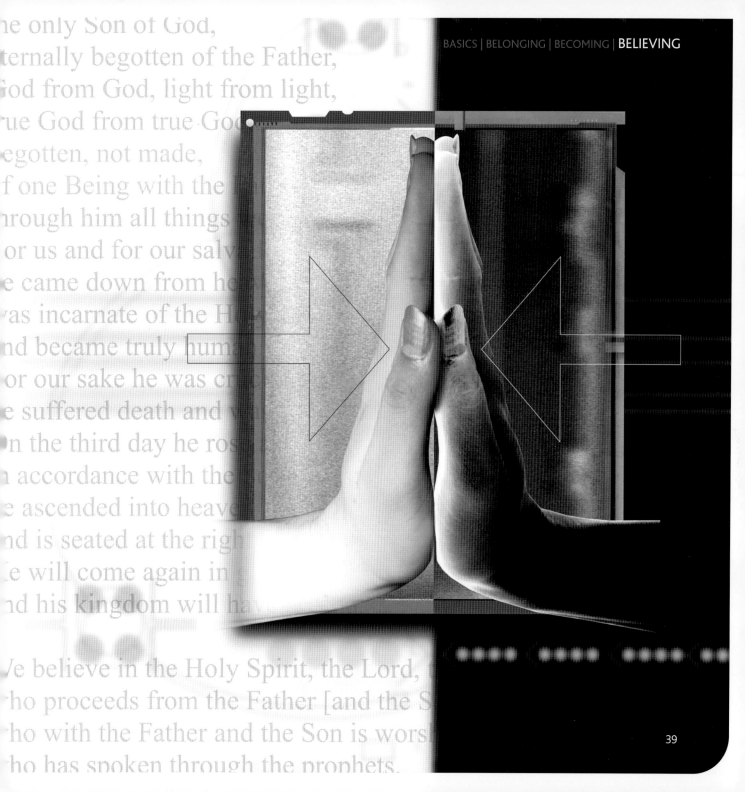

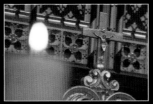 

Why, in our services, do we tell God so much he knows already? Psalms, hymns and prayers describe in detail either what God is like – good, faithful and so on – or what God did for us long ago in the Bible. Surely God can't have forgotten all this? So why do we keep on reminding him?

Talking about God, telling God's story is the way we praise him. We do this out loud to remind ourselves and anyone listening that God rescued us through his extraordinary love. We couldn't have done it by ourselves. In other words, we are giving credit where credit is due – to God. When we tell the story that shows God to be the hero, he gets the praise and glory he deserves.

PRAISE AND THANKSGIVING

And when we do, we are not just buttering God up with fine words to get what we want – even though it might sound like that sometimes. It's not the same as flattering a rich aunt from whom we hope to borrow money – admiring her dress, possessions and youthful appearance, to put her in a good mood before we get down to the real business of our visit! Our praise and thanksgiving is not just a prelude to our prayer. It is the foundation on which all our praying is built. It changes the way we see things. It focuses us on God as the source and centre of our lives.

Because God is the same yesterday, today and for ever, recalling what he did for us in the past gives us confidence to expect him to act in similar ways in the present and the future. Telling God's story reminds us what we can ask him to do for us – and what we should not expect him to do. When prayers start with what we want instead of remembering what God wants, they can go off course.

Glory to the Father, the God of love, who created us;
who continually preserves and sustains us;
who has loved us with an everlasting love,
and given us the light of the knowledge of his glory
in the face of Jesus Christ.
Blessed be God for ever.

New Patterns for Worship

FORETASTE OF HEAVEN?

Amazingly, after all these years Enid Blyton's books are as popular as they ever were – and not just with children. Most of us can remember at least parts of the stories we read long ago. Among the images that stick in our minds are the food, pop and 'lashings of ginger beer' that the children always seemed to take with them whenever they set off on an adventure, and the superb feast they would make somewhere along the way. Just thinking about it can make our mouths water, wanting to be there, sharing the feast with them.

The Holy Communion may not look much like that sort of feast but the bread and wine do represent the lavish banquet God has prepared for us in heaven, where he has set a place for each one of us. When we celebrate the Eucharist together, we are not just recalling a past event – however crucial for our salvation that event was – we are also looking forward to the future. Remembering the past, we make it a present reality; picturing the future, we have a foretaste of it here and now. Our gathering around the Lord's Table is a symbol of God's desire to gather and feed all people with his goodness.

In the Eucharist, past, present and future meet. This vision calls us to work with God to bring about his rule on earth, as it is in heaven. As our spiritual hunger is satisfied, we must remember those who have no daily bread and those who eat the bread of affliction. This act of worship should make us long for all to share the lavish feast. It should make our mouths water.

Finish then thy new creation,
Pure and spotless let us be;
Let us see thy great salvation,
Perfectly restored in thee:
Changed from glory into glory,
Till in heaven we take our place,
Till we cast our crowns before thee,
Lost in wonder, love, and praise!

Charles Wesley

THE OFFICE

In these days of reality television, the BBC had an unlikely hit with the 2005 series *The Monastery*. A group of men lived with a monastic community and shared their way of life for forty days. Believers, spiritual searchers and those with no religious background, they joined in 'the office', the daily round of prayer: sometimes they struggled and sometimes they made astonishing personal breakthroughs.

As a result, the abbey reported an unexpected upsurge of interest in this ancient pattern of prayer throughout the day – the team there now runs regular retreats for men and women in search of answers to life's big questions. Yet this popularity shouldn't surprise us: a pattern of daily praying has underpinned Christianity from its earliest days, as it has other faiths.

Within the Church of England, *The Book of Common Prayer* has always expected Morning and Evening Prayer (the Daily Office) to be said or sung daily. Forms of Daily Prayer in *Common Worship* continue the tradition. In an age where patterns of work and leisure are distorted by the '24/7' culture, many people feel the need to have familiar signposts to mark out the progression of time in their day.

A regular, disciplined pattern of praying, with other believers and on our own, helps strengthen our belief in God, enables us to share in Jesus' heavenly work of praise and prayer, and allows us short periods of retreat each day to reflect on our walk with God.

O Lord, open thou our lips
and our mouth shall shew forth thy praise.

O God, make speed to save us.
O Lord, make haste to help us.

The Book of Common Prayer

MISSION-SHAPED WORSHIP

Many people think of going to church each week as a chance to withdraw from the world to recharge spiritual batteries before going back for another seven days.

It's like Jesus going up on to a mountain to pray before coming down to continue his mission, or the time he spent in the Garden of Gethsemane before facing those who came to arrest him and put him to death. We retreat in order to re-group so that, in turn, we can better advance. That makes a great deal of sense.

But there is another way to think of times of worship: not as a temporary retreat from the mission Jesus gives us, but actually as part of our engagement in God's mission to the world. Rather than being entirely inward-looking, our worship can also be outward-looking and prophetic.

A congregation that sees its worship as part of God's mission will find that its intercessory prayers are not just for the church, the needs of their own congregation and people they know and love. They will be for the wider world, for justice for oppressed peoples every-where, for peace in war-torn areas; indeed, for the whole of God's creation.

A congregation that sees its worship as part of God's mission welcomes every newcomer, whatever their race or background, and helps them feel at home. Members talk to strangers and invite them to refreshments after the service. They may choose to include more popular music and simpler prayers or make some provision for babies and young children so parents can relax.

Above all, a congregation that sees its worship as part of God's mission will be a baptizing community. They won't relegate baptisms to Sunday afternoons so their own service is undisturbed. They won't see baptism as solely the responsibility of the priest but as a normal and natural part of what it is to be a follower of Jesus.

Making the most of celebrating baptism can transform lives – in candidates, in families and friends, and even in regular members of the congregation.

And a church with this sort of transforming worship at its heart will be a missionary church.

Go therefore and make disciples of all
nations, baptizing them in the name of
the Father and of the Son and of the
Holy Spirit . . . And remember, I am
with you always, to the end of the age.

Matthew 28.19

ACKNOWLEDGEMENTS

The editors would like to express their particular gratitude to Kathryn Pritchard of Church House Publishing for her patience, good humour and wisdom in the writing of this book.

The publisher gratefully acknowledges permission to reproduce copyright material in this book. Every effort has been made to trace and contact copyright holders. If there are any inadvertent omissions we apologize to those concerned and undertake to include suitable acknowledgements in all future editions.

Thanks are due to the following for permission to reproduce copyright material:

Cambridge University Press: extracts (and adapted extracts) from *The Book of Common Prayer*, the rights in which are vested in the Crown, are reproduced by permission of the Crown's Patentee, Cambridge University Press.

GIA Publications Inc. Chicago, USA (www.giamusic.com): verse (p. 22) from Marty Haugen's hymn 'Let us build a house'. All rights reserved. Used by permission.

Kingsway Communications Ltd: David Evans text (p.17) adm. by worshiptogether.com.songs excl. UK & Europe, adm. by kingswaysongs.com; tym@kingsway.co.uk

The Methodist Publishing House: prayer (p. 41) from The *Methodist Worship Book* © 1999 Trustees for Methodist Church Purposes.

Erik Routley's prayer (p. 36) 'God of glory, around whose throne...' was composed for Westminster Choir College (Princeton).

Photography: Copyright material supplied by Fresh Expressions, Getty Images, Jupiter Images, Kippa Matthews, Marcus Perkins, Leo Sorel, Tim Stratford, Trevillion Trinity Wall Street and Veer, reproduced by permission.